Stars

Fiction and Nonfiction Paired Reading

Always Looking Up
LAURA GEHL

Stars
Linda Aspen-Baxter

Fiction and Nonfiction Paired Reading

Go to www.openlightbox.com and enter this book's unique code.

BOOK CODE

AVN43742

Explore your **AV2 Fiction** interactive eBook!

This empowering picture book biography tells the story of Nancy Grace Roman, the astronomer who overcame obstacles like weak eyesight and teachers who discouraged women from pursuing astronomy to lead the NASA team that built the Hubble Space Telescope.

Always Looking Up
First Published by

The Benefits of Paired Fiction and Nonfiction

Pairing fiction and nonfiction titles is a research-based educational approach proven to enhance student outcomes. It improves reading comprehension, increases engagement, expands background knowledge, and helps build vocabulary.

Each paired fiction title is read aloud by professional narrators, offering students the opportunity to listen and learn at their own pace. Every paired nonfiction title comes with a host of digital features designed to engage all learning styles and build a solid foundation for future growth. Both fiction and nonfiction titles are sure to captivate even the most reluctant reader with their dynamic visuals and curated content.

AV2 Fiction Readalong Navigation

1-Year Grades K–5 Premium Fiction Subscription ISBN
979-8-8745-1655-0

The digital components of this book are guaranteed to stay active for at least five years from the date of publication.

ALWAYS LOOKING UP

NANCY GRACE ROMAN, ASTRONOMER

Young Nancy Grace loved to look up at the endless night sky. She gazed at tiny blue-white stars glittering in inky blackness.

Her father's job changed again and again. For Nancy Grace, this meant moving from Tennessee to Texas, to Oklahoma, to New Jersey, then to Michigan. Each new place seemed different and strange.

But the same night sky extended across the country and beyond. Nancy Grace looked up to see the familiar moon glowing above each new home.

And wearing her first pair of glasses, Nancy Grace looked up through their lenses to see colors twirling and dancing on a dark stage—the northern lights.

With curiosity as boundless as the universe, Nancy Grace vowed to learn more about space. She gathered friends into an astronomy club to study the constellations. Together, they mapped sparkling patterns on an infinite black canvas.

Standing in the quiet night, Nancy Grace watched brilliant meteors shoot across an ocean of deep dark blue. And she noticed Venus and Jupiter, outshining the stars.

Nancy Grace read every astronomy book in the public library.

But then her eyes grew weak, and the doctor ordered a break: no reading except for schoolwork.

Still, no one could stop Nancy Grace from reading the night sky.

And she was unstoppable at school, where she tutored a fellow student in math, asked questions her physics teacher could not answer, and requested a second algebra class instead of Latin.

"What *lady* would take mathematics instead of Latin?" the guidance counselor asked.

A lady planning to be an astronomer, that's who!

With determination as fiery as a supernova, Nancy Grace went on to college, where her professors told her science and math were masculine subjects. Cold hard facts and calculations were best left to men, they believed. Literature and history, those were for women.

Yet Nancy Grace knew astronomy was for her.

And her eyes were strong again—strong enough to read a tower of books stretching toward space. Nancy Grace blazed through science classes until one teacher admitted, "Maybe you just might make it."

Nancy Grace zoomed ahead to graduate school. Some teachers did not approve of women pursuing advanced degrees. They thought women should leave school and get married instead.

But Nancy Grace stayed focused on the stars of the Big Dipper, studying their movements through space.

She still looked up at the sky every night—but now it was her job. Nancy Grace had pushed past everyone steering her toward "ladylike" careers, such as teaching or nursing. She had achieved her goal of becoming an astronomer.

Yet this was only the beginning.

With powerful tools and her powerful mind, astronomer Nancy Grace searched for new information, new answers, even new questions about the universe.

She studied bright stars in our swirly Milky Way, noting that young stars moved differently from older ones.

She observed binary stars, like AG Draconis—a giant star and a dwarf star orbiting each other.

She worked with radio telescopes, detecting invisible energy from stars and planets.

Her research spread across the world to astronomers in the Soviet Union—where Americans were not normally welcome. They read Nancy Grace's published paper about AG Draconis and invited her to visit.

Nancy Grace's trip intrigued other scientists. She gave a talk when she returned to the US, then a series of ten astronomy lectures.

Nancy Grace's passion shone as she spoke. She had seen and learned so much in her career already. Now she could share that knowledge with others.

When brand-new NASA needed a chief of astronomy, Nancy Grace seized the opportunity.

She traveled the country, asking scientists about their hopes for space astronomy. Many had the same desire: a clear view of space from above the atmosphere. Nancy Grace understood that the atmosphere blocks and alters light from space. "Looking at stars through the atmosphere," she wrote in an essay, "is not too different from looking at streetlights through a pane of old stained glass."

Nancy Grace dreamed of helping astronomers see farther into space than humans had ever seen before—past the moon, past Venus and Jupiter, past the stars she had mapped as a child.

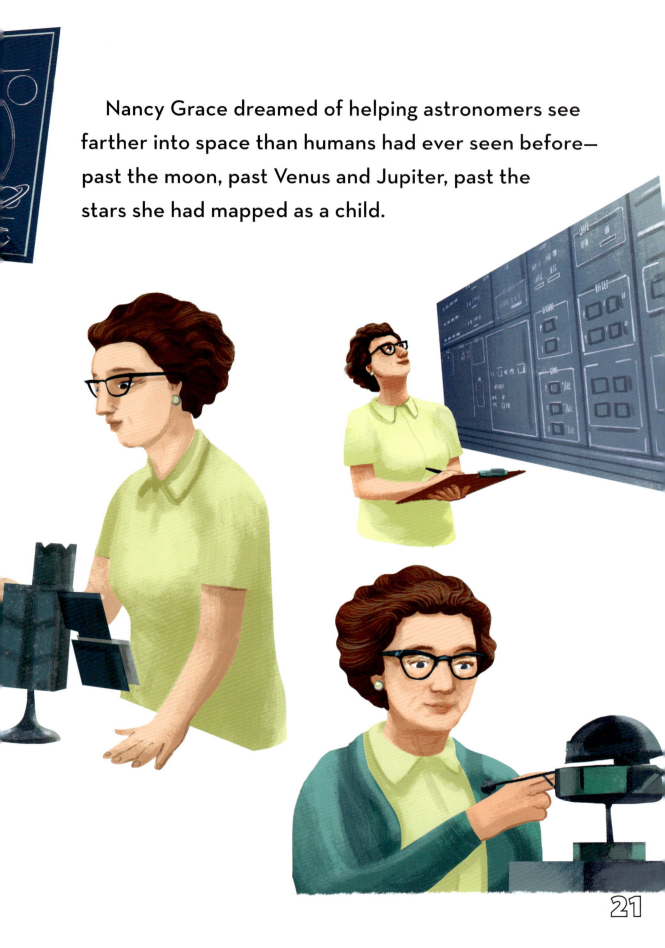

The world needed a new kind of telescope: one that floated above the atmosphere, orbiting Earth while capturing images of infant stars, black holes, and galaxies billions of light-years away.

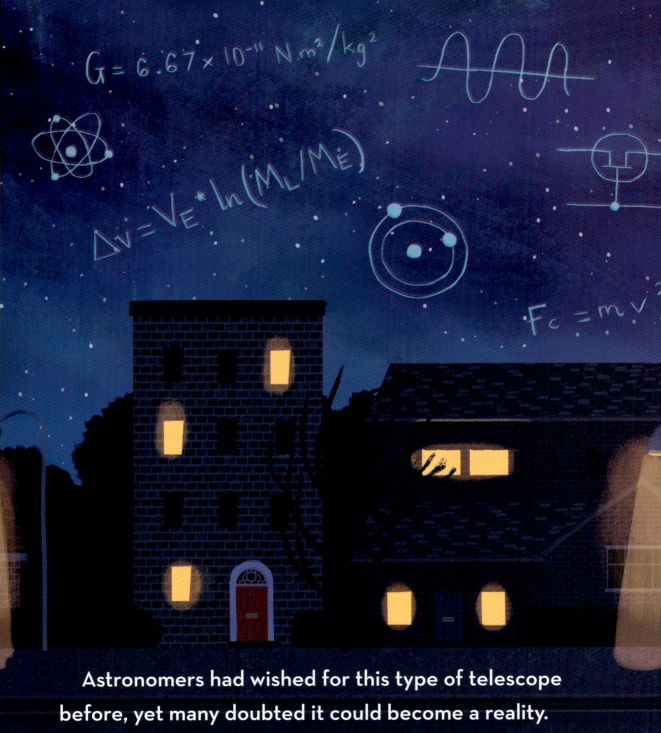

Astronomers had wished for this type of telescope before, yet many doubted it could become a reality. A large space telescope would cost millions, maybe billions of dollars. It would be difficult to build. Telescopes on Earth were good enough.

But Nancy Grace had faced doubters before.

She brought astronomers and engineers together. What did astronomers want? What did engineers believe possible? What if something went wrong up in space? Meetings continued for years. Gradually, they agreed on a design. A design that would become the Hubble Space Telescope.

NASA needed money from Congress to pay for Hubble—lots of money. One senator questioned whether taxpayers should fund an expensive telescope. But Nancy Grace had experience defending her choices.

"For the price of a single night at the movies, every American…will get fifteen years of exciting scientific results," she wrote in response.

Finally, more than a decade later—following design changes, delays, and setbacks—a shuttle carried Hubble into space. As big as a bus, as heavy as two elephants, Hubble was launched into orbit.

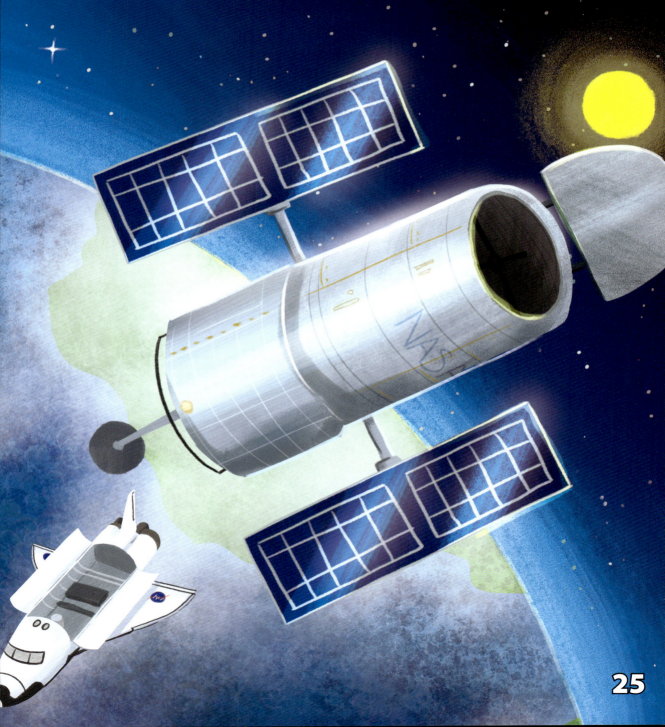

The world waited for the first photographs taken without the distortion of the atmosphere. Photographs that would prove Hubble worthy of the money and years of effort.

But the first images were blurry. And hopes plummeted like a falling meteorite.

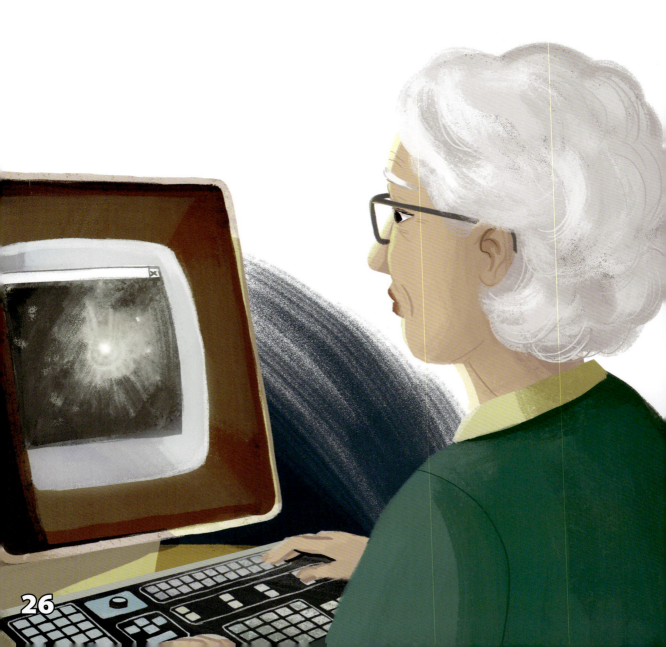

Yet, way back when Nancy Grace brought a team together to design Hubble, they had repair missions in mind. Hubble was the first telescope designed to be serviced in space.

Three years after Hubble's launch, astronauts installed a device to correct the faulty mirror. It was like putting "glasses" on Hubble.

Once again, people across the globe waited for pictures. Would the fix work? Nancy Grace waited too.

Yes!

Crystal clear images from Hubble dazzled and delighted, informed and inspired.

Nancy Grace, called "Mother of Hubble," marveled along with the rest of the world at the photographs sent back from space—comets hurtling into Jupiter; dust storms on Mars; nebulae shaped like a butterfly, a crab, a tarantula.

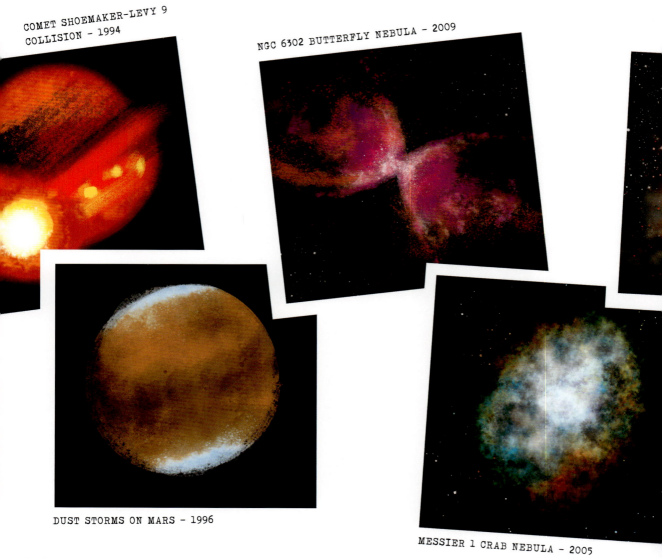

COMET SHOEMAKER-LEVY 9 COLLISION - 1994

NGC 6302 BUTTERFLY NEBULA - 2009

DUST STORMS ON MARS - 1996

MESSIER 1 CRAB NEBULA - 2005

28

Over the next quarter of a century—much longer than the fifteen years Nancy Grace had promised Congress—Hubble changed the way people saw the universe, and helped scientists make giant leaps in understanding space. Astronomers could track the shrinking red spot on Jupiter, measure the atmosphere of planets beyond our solar system, and estimate the age of the universe.

NGC 2060
TARANTULA NEBULA - 2011

JUPITER'S GREAT RED SPOT
AND GANYMEDE'S SHADOW - 2014

NGC 922 - 2012

IC 63 GHOST NEBULA - 2018

After retiring, Nancy Grace never stopped learning about astronomy—reading papers, attending lectures, talking with other astronomers. And even in her nineties, Nancy Grace loved to walk outside and look up at the endless night sky. As she said, "The real way to learn about the sky is to look at it."

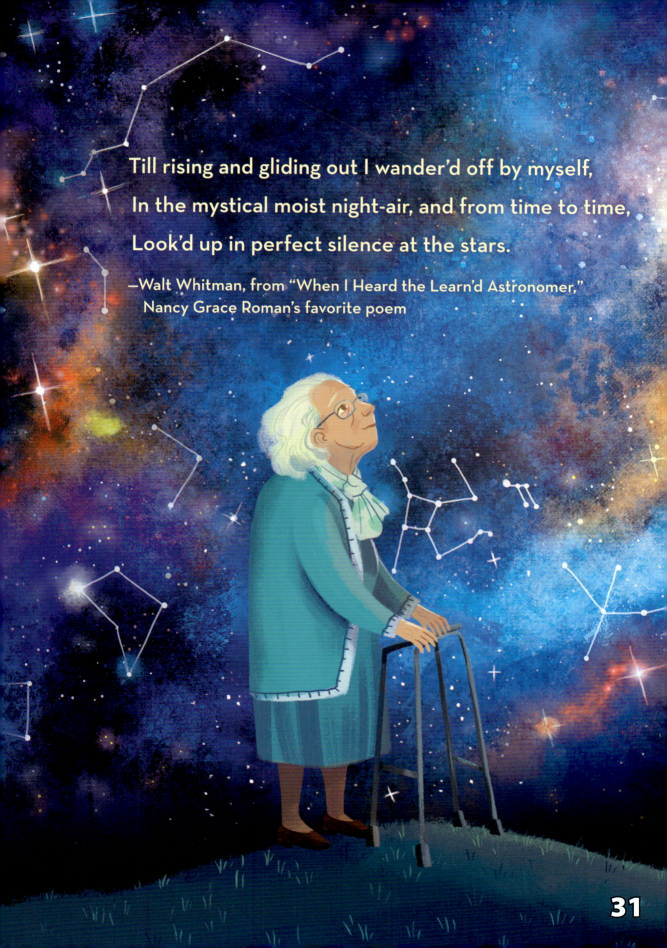

Till rising and gliding out I wander'd off by myself,
In the mystical moist night-air, and from time to time,
Look'd up in perfect silence at the stars.

—Walt Whitman, from "When I Heard the Learn'd Astronomer," Nancy Grace Roman's favorite poem

AUTHOR'S NOTE

Many people over many decades worked to make the Hubble Space Telescope a reality. But only Nancy Grace earned the nickname "Mother of Hubble." Nancy Grace Roman, who struggled with weak eyesight as a child, helped astronomers—and everyone else on Earth—see farther into space than ever before.

While Nancy Grace is most famous as the "Mother of Hubble," her proudest accomplishment was launching a much smaller telescope into orbit. This telescope, called the International Ultraviolet Explorer (IUE), did not take pictures. Nobody outside of the astronomy community knew or cared about its launch in 1978. But the IUE gave astronomers information about the wavelengths of ultraviolet light from objects in space. Scientists could not get that data from a ground-based telescope, because Earth's ozone layer blocks the UV wavelengths. Nancy Grace fought for this little satellite just like she fought for giant Hubble. And thanks to Nancy Grace, scientists have published more than five thousand research papers using data from the IUE.

While Nancy Grace was lucky her childhood problems with weak eyesight did not persist into adulthood, she never forgot those years when she was not allowed to read. After her retirement, Nancy Grace read astronomy books aloud for adults with dyslexia and impaired vision.

Nancy Grace also enjoyed talking with students and offered advice to kids who love science:
1. If you are a girl or a boy who wants to be a scientist, go for it!
2. Be flexible. Your career may lead you in unexpected directions.
3. Science is changing all the time, which means the right job for you might not even exist yet.

TIMELINE

1925 — Nancy Grace Roman is born in Nashville, Tennessee.

1929 — Edwin Hubble formulates Hubble's Law, leading to acceptance of the idea that the universe is expanding.

1935 — Between fifth and sixth grade, Nancy Grace organizes her friends into an astronomy club.

1937 — Seventh-grader Nancy Grace, having read every astronomy book in the public library, decides she will be an astronomer.

1946 — Nancy Grace graduates from Swarthmore College with a BA in astronomy.

1949 — Nancy Grace receives her PhD in astronomy from the University of Chicago. She continues her teaching and research at the University of Chicago until 1955.

1955 — Nancy Grace takes a job in radio astronomy at the US Naval Research Laboratory.

1957 — The Soviet Union launches Sputnik I, the first human-made Earth-orbiting satellite, igniting the space race between the Soviet Union and the United States.

1958 — The United States creates the National Aeronautics and Space Administration (NASA).

1959 — Nancy Grace joins NASA at its headquarters to develop a program in space astronomy. Her title will become Chief of Astronomy and Relativity Programs.

1961 — Yuri Gagarin, Soviet cosmonaut, becomes the first person in space. Alan Shepard Jr. becomes the first American astronaut in space shortly afterward.

1969 — Neil Armstrong becomes the first person to walk on the moon. Nancy Grace receives the NASA Exceptional Scientific Achievement Medal.

1977 — Congress approves funding for the Hubble Space Telescope, in large part due to Nancy Grace's efforts.

1978 — Nancy Grace receives the NASA Outstanding Leadership Medal.

1979 — Nancy Grace retires from NASA to take care of her mother. She continues working on the Hubble Space Telescope and other astronomical projects as a consultant.

1983 — Sally Ride becomes the first female American astronaut in space. NASA flies Nancy Grace to Florida for the launch.

1986 — An asteroid is named 2516 Roman, after Nancy Grace. The space shuttle *Challenger* disaster delays Hubble's launch by several years.

1990 — The Hubble Space Telescope is put into orbit. Blurry images transmitted back to Earth reveal a problem with the telescope's mirror.

1993 — Astronauts repair Hubble in a series of space walks. Hubble begins to send crystal clear photographs back to Earth.

1995 — Nancy Grace becomes director of the Astronomical Data Center at NASA's Goddard Space Flight Center.

1997 — Nancy Grace retires for the second time.

2011 — NASA establishes the Nancy Grace Roman Technology Fellowship in Astrophysics.

2018 — Nancy Grace Roman passes away at the age of 93.

Fiction and Nonfiction Paired Reading

Go to www.openlightbox.com and enter this book's unique code.

BOOK CODE

AVN43742

Explore your **AV2 Nonfiction** interactive eBook!

Did you know that stars last for billions of years? Some stars shrink and turn white when they are very old. Find out more in *Stars*, a title in the **Discovering Space** series.

Stars
First Published by

34

AV2 is optimized for use on any device

AV2 Nonfiction Readalong Navigation

 Contents Browse a live contents page to easily navigate through resources

 Audio Listen to sections of the book read aloud

 Videos Watch informative video clips

 Weblinks Gain additional information for research

 Slideshows View images and captions

 Try This! Complete activities and hands-on experiments

 Key Words Study vocabulary, and complete a matching word activity

 Quizzes Test your knowledge

 Share Share titles within your Learning Management System (LMS) or Library Circulation System

 Citation Create bibliographical references following APA, CMOS, and MLA styles

1-Year Grades K–5 Premium Fiction Subscription ISBN
979-8-8745-1655-0

The digital components of this book are guaranteed to stay active for at least five years from the date of publication.

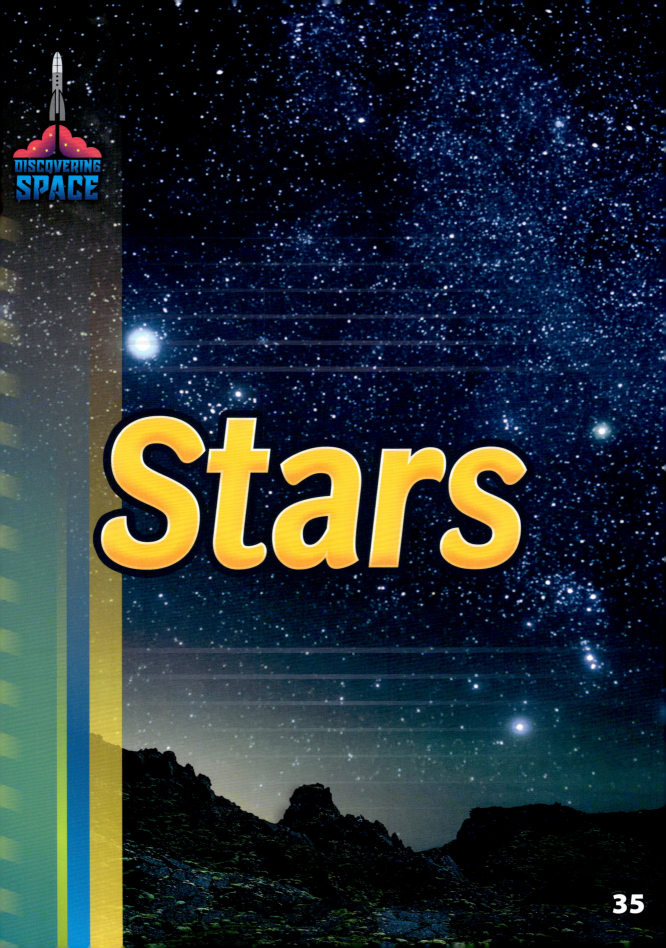

Stars

Twinkling Stars

Stars twinkle in the night sky. Their light comes from very far away. Stars are made of **gas** and dust. They appear small from Earth because they are so far away. In fact, stars are very large. Some stars are even larger than Earth's Sun. The **mass** of some stars can be about 10 times greater than that of the Sun. Other stars are much smaller.

Star Diameter Size Comparison

Betelgeuse
860 million miles
(1.4 billion kilometers)

Aldebaran
38 million miles (61 million km)

Arcturus
22 million miles (35 million km)

Sun
864,000 miles (1.4 million km)

Proxima Centauri
120,000 miles (193,000 km)

Earth's Closest Star

The Sun is the closest star to Earth. It takes eight minutes for the Sun's light to reach Earth. Earth is about 93 million miles (150 million kilometers) from the Sun. Light from other stars takes longer to reach Earth because these stars are so much farther away. After the Sun, the closest star to Earth is Proxima Centauri.

The light from **Proxima Centauri** takes **4.2 years** to reach Earth.

Long Lives

Stars live for billions of years. They cool and change color over time. **Energy** flows from the middle of a star. This keeps the star bright. Stars are classified according to their color and luminosity, or brightness.

Some stars appear less bright than they really are because they are farther away than other stars. The larger a star's mass, the shorter its life will be.

Star Colors

The Sun is a yellow star. It will change into a red star when it begins to cool. Stars vary in color. The color they **emit** is based on their **temperature**.

The Sun is a type of star called a yellow dwarf. As it cools, it will expand into a red giant before turning white.

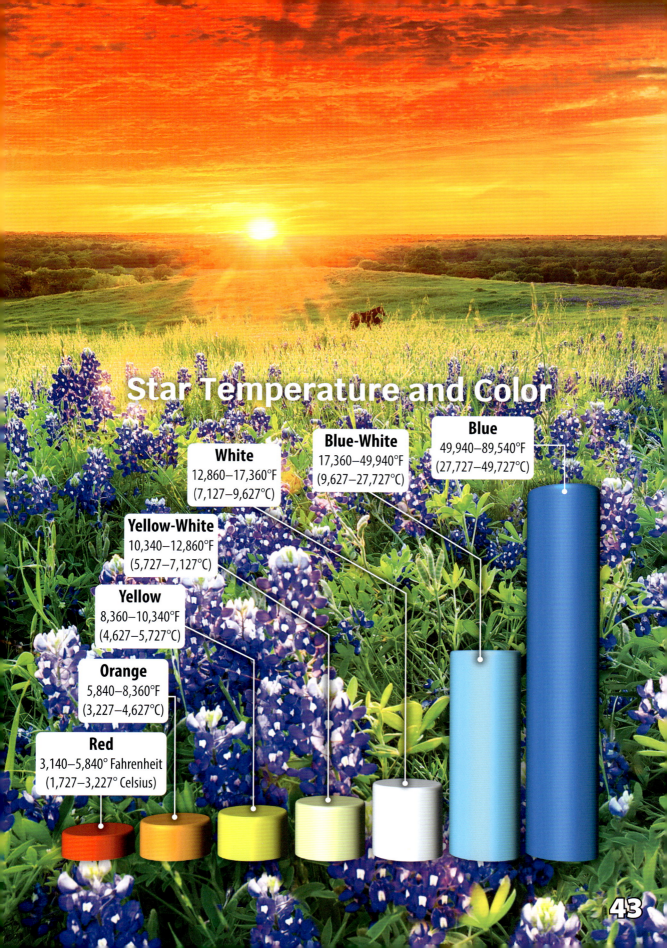

Growing Old

Some stars shrink and turn white when they are very old. They turn black when they have stopped cooling.

When stars first begin to cool, they may actually grow in size. As they burn off their gases, they begin to shed layers. Most stars eventually die after turning black.

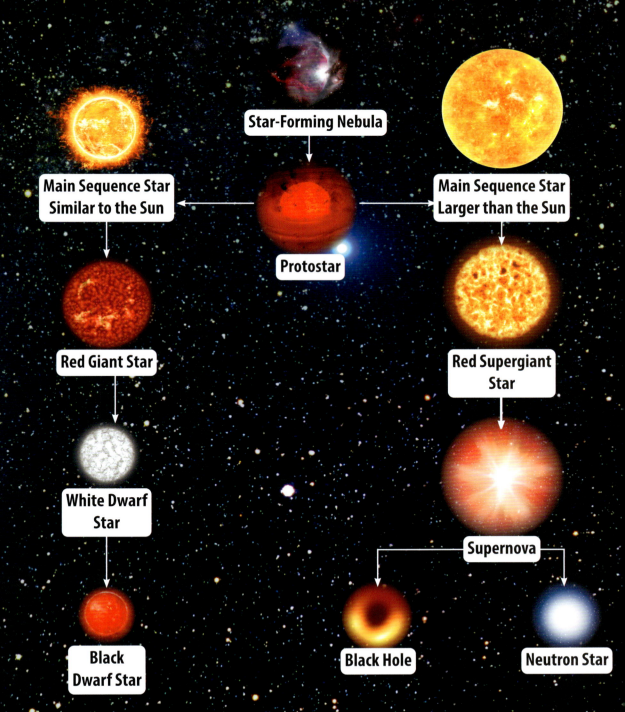

When Stars Explode

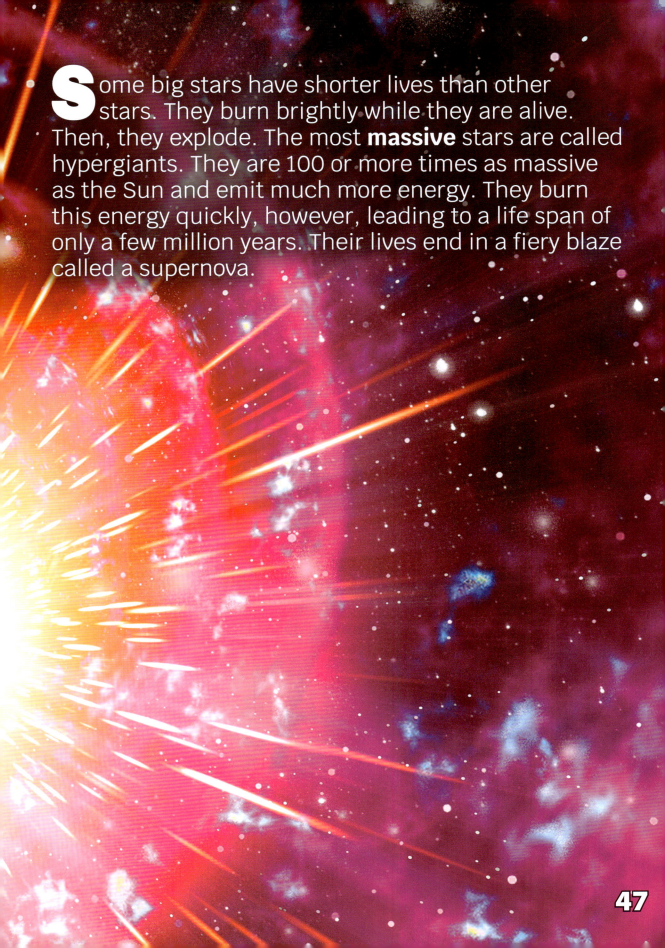

Some big stars have shorter lives than other stars. They burn brightly while they are alive. Then, they explode. The most **massive** stars are called hypergiants. They are 100 or more times as massive as the Sun and emit much more energy. They burn this energy quickly, however, leading to a life span of only a few million years. Their lives end in a fiery blaze called a supernova.

47

The Night Sky

It is easy to see stars from Earth when the sky is dark. Fewer stars can be seen when the Moon is full. Stargazers often travel to dark-sky locations, far away from city lights, to view the night sky. City lights can block star **visibility** up to 200 miles (322 km) away.

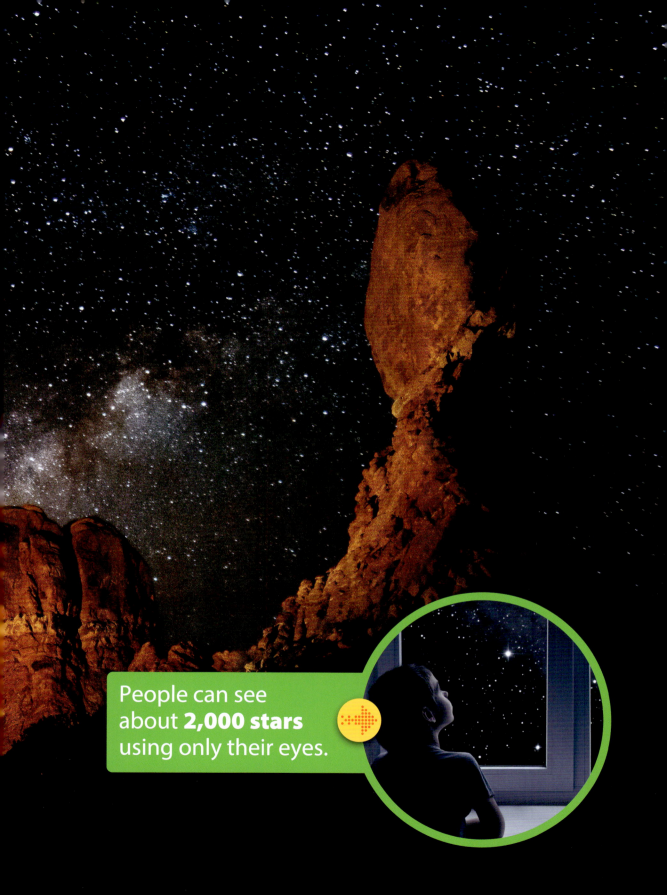

People can see about **2,000 stars** using only their eyes.

49

Star Shapes

A group of stars can form a shape in the sky. This shape is called a constellation. People in ancient times saw patterns when they looked up at the twinkling skies. They imagined lines that connected the stars. These lines formed shapes that are now called constellations.

There are 88 different constellations in the sky. People in the northern **hemisphere** see different constellations than people in the southern hemisphere. Travelers in the past used constellations to find their way across land and sea.

Northern Hemisphere

In the northern hemisphere, the Little Dipper, part of the Ursa Minor constellation, contains a star called Polaris. This star is the closest to the celestial North Pole.

Southern Hemisphere

In the southern hemisphere, the Southern Cross, belonging to the Crux constellation, was used to find South. Its longer bar joins the stars Gacrux and Acrux and points to the celestial South Pole.

Stargazing

People sometimes use a **telescope** to look at stars in the night sky. No one knows for sure how many stars there are. Like many stargazers, astronomers use telescopes to see distant stars. These large telescopes are housed in buildings called observatories. Arizona's Lowell Observatory, established in 1894, is one of the oldest observatories in the United States.

Some people travel to **Flagstaff, Arizona**, for a clear view of the stars in the night sky.

Star Quiz

1 What color are the hottest stars?

2 What is Earth's closest star?

3 What is the name of the most massive stars?

4 What type of star is the Sun?

5 What is the name of the shape a group of stars can form in the sky?

6 What are the buildings that house large telescopes called?

7 When was Arizona's Lowell Observatory established?

8 How many stars can people see using only their eyes?

ANSWERS
1. Blue **2.** The Sun **3.** Hypergiants **4.** A yellow dwarf **5.** Constellation **6.** Observatories **7.** 1894 **8.** About 2,000

Key Words

emit: release something such as light or heat

energy: usable power

gas: a substance that can expand, unlike solid or liquid substances

hemisphere: half of a planet, such as Earth

mass: a measurement of the amount of matter in an object

massive: remarkably large or heavy

telescope: a tool with a system of mirrors or lenses used to view distant objects

temperature: degree of hotness or coldness of an object

visibility: the ability to be easily seen

Index (Nonfiction)

Aldebaran 37
Arcturus 37

Betelgeuse 37

color 40, 42, 43
constellation 50, 51, 54

dust 36

gas 36, 45

Earth 36, 38, 39, 48, 54
energy 40, 47

hemisphere 51
hypergiants 47, 54

Lowell Observatory 52
luminosity 40

Moon 48

Proxima Centauri 37, 38, 39

red giant 42, 45

Sun 36, 37, 38, 42, 45, 47, 54
supernova 45, 47

telescope 52
temperature 42, 43

yellow dwarf 42, 54

Get the best of both worlds.

AV2 bridges the gap between print and digital.

The expandable resources toolbar enables quick access to content including **videos**, **audio**, **activities**, **weblinks**, **slideshows**, **quizzes**, and **key words**.

Animated videos make static images come alive.

Resource icons on each page help readers to further **explore key concepts**.

Published by Lightbox Learning Inc.
276 5th Avenue, Suite 704 #917
New York, NY 10001
Website: www.openlightbox.com

Always Looking Up
First Published by
Albert Whitman & Co.

Stars
First Published by
AV2

Always Looking Up
Written by Laura Gehl, illustrated by Louise Pigott and Alex Oxton
Text copyright ©2019 by Laura Gehl
Illustrations copyright ©2019 by Albert Whitman & Company
Published by arrangement with Albert Whitman & Company
First published in the United States of America in 2019 by Albert Whitman & Company, 250 South Northwest Highway, Suite 320, Park Ridge, Illinois 60068 USA
ALL RIGHTS RESERVED

Lightbox Learning acknowledges Getty Images as the primary image supplier for the AV2 *Stars* title.

Copyright ©2026 Lightbox Learning Inc.
All rights reserved. No part of this publication may be reproduced, stored in a retrieval system, or transmitted in any form or by any means, electronic, mechanical, photocopying, recording, or otherwise, without the prior written permission of the publisher.

Library of Congress Control Number: 2024948027

ISBN 979-8-8745-1954-4 (hardcover)
ISBN 979-8-8745-1953-7 (softcover)
ISBN 979-8-8745-1952-0 (multi-user static eBook)
ISBN 979-8-8745-1950-6 (multi-user interactive eBook)

Printed in Guangzhou, China
1 2 3 4 5 6 7 8 9 0   28 27 26 25 24

112024
102724

Project Coordinator: Priyanka Das
Art Director: Terry Paulhus
Layout: Jean Faye Rodriguez

These titles are part of our Premium Fiction digital subscription

1-Year Grades K–5 Premium Fiction Subscription ISBN
979-8-8745-1655-0

Access dozens of Paired Reading and Storytime titles with our Premium Fiction digital subscription.
Sign up for a FREE trial at **www.openlightbox.com/trial**